Gastric Sleeve Cookbook®:

Carefully Selected Easy to Make Recipes:
Healthy and Delicious for LEGENDS
After Gastric Surgery
All the Best Have Lovely Taste!

Amy Wilson

Table of Contents

Introduction

Congratulations on downloading Gastric Sleeve Cookbook (R): Carefully Selected Easy to Make Recipes; Healthy and Delicious for LEGENDS After Gastric Surgery. All The Best Have Lovely Taste!

Thank you for doing so.

The following chapters will discuss many recipes that can change the way you prepare your meals. You will want to maintain a good weight loss program. Each one of these meals has all the essential information to incorporate them into your new way of life.

There are plenty of books on this subject on the market, thanks again for choosing this one! Every effort was made to ensure it is full of as much useful information as possible. Please enjoy!

Chapter 1: Breakfast Goodies

Crustless Quiche

Servings: 6
Calories: 106.8
Prep and Cooking Time: 00:50:00

Ingredients
- 2 c egg beaters/egg whites
- 1 c cottage cheese (non-fat)
- ½ c each:
  - Chopped – cooked broccoli
  - Diced lean ham
- Colby or cheddar shredded cheese
- Cooking spray
- Pepper and salt to taste

Instructions
1. Set the oven temperature to 375°F. Spray a casserole dish with the cooking spray and add all of the ingredients.
2. Bake until the center is set (45 minutes).

Sausage and Mushroom Gravy

Servings: 4
Calories: 115.4
Prep and Cooking Time: 00:17

Ingredients
- 8 ounces/2 c chopped mushrooms**
- ¼ large chopped onions
- 2 tbsp each:
    - Olive oil
    - Whole wheat flour
- ¼ tsp each:
    - Black pepper
    - Red pepper flakes
    - Dried sage
- ½ tsp dried thyme
- 1 ½ c skim milk
  **For best results use the white button or baby bella mushrooms.

Instructions
1. Place the oil and onions in a sauté pan. After two minutes, toss in the mushrooms and continue cooking another three to four minutes.
2. Fold in the flour, mixing for one minute, and combine with the spices.
3. Gently, empty in the milk, stirring until the sauce is creamy. Simmer about five more minutes

Eggs

Baked Egg Cups

Servings: 6
Calories: 125.6
Prep and Cooking Time: 00:30:00

Ingredients
- 6 eggs
- 6 slices deli ham – lean
- ½ c 2% cheddar cheese – shredded
- 1 tbsp chopped chives
- Pepper
- Non-stick cooking spray

Instructions
1. Set the oven temperature at 350°F.
2. Lightly spray six muffin tins and arrange the ham slices to line the cup. Bake ten minutes.
3. Take the tins out of the oven and add an egg to each cup.
4. Break the yolk and add a sprinkle of pepper.
5. Bake another ten minutes if they are done to your preference. Garnish with cheese and chives.

Egg in a Basket

Servings: 1
Calories: 246.2
Prep and Cooking Time: 00:15

Ingredients
- 1 large egg
- 1 slice of bread
- Butter flavored cooking spray

Instructions
1. Remove the middle out of the slice of bread using a glass.
2. Use some cooking spray on a griddle with the

medium heat setting.
3. Arrange the bread on the skillet/griddle and add the broken egg.
4. Cook until done.

Eggs and Oats

Servings: 1
Calories: 272.6
Prep and Cooking Time: 00:10:00

Ingredients
- 2 egg whites
- 1 whole egg
- 2 ounces skim milk
- ½ c rolled oats (Quaker)
- *Optional Garnishes:*
  - Hot sauce
  - Cayenne
  - Honey cinnamon berries

Instructions
1. Use some non-stick cooking spray to lightly grease a skillet. Add all of the ingredients.
2. Cook as with any scrambled egg.

Sausage and Egg Casserole

Servings: 12
Calories: 200.5
Prep and Cooking Time: 00:40

Ingredients
- 12 large eggs

- ¼ c skim milk
- 12 ounces breakfast sausage – browned
- ¼ tsp pepper
- 2 c low-fat cheddar shredded cheese

Instructions
1. Program the oven temperature to 375°F.
2. Mix all of the components and empty the mixture into a lightly greased 12-c muffin pan.
3. Bake 30 minutes, cool for five, and serve.

Note: This can also be baked in a casserole dish.

Spinach and Feta Egg Whites

Servings: 1
Calories: 200.3
Prep and Cooking Time: 00:15:00

Ingredients
- 2 c baby spinach
- 3 egg whites
- 1 chopped tomato
- ¼ c each:
  - Chopped onion
  - Crumbled feta cheese

Instructions
1. Chop the veggies and add them in a pan to cook using medium heat, cooking the onions until they are translucent.
2. Add the spinach, tomato, and egg whites. Blend in the ½ of the cheese.

3. Garnish the top with the remainder of cheese, pepper, and salt.

Muffins and Breakfast Cookies

Blueberry Muffin

Servings: 12
Calories: 102.8
Prep and Cooking Time: 00:35

Ingredients
- ½ tsp. salt
- 1 c of each:
  - Flour
  - Old-fashioned oats
- 1 tsp. each:
  - Baking soda
  - Cinnamon
- ½ c each:
  - Unsweetened applesauce
  - Water
  - Sugar
- 2 egg whites
- 1 c frozen blueberries

Instructions
1. Prepare 12 muffin tins and program the oven to 350°F.
2. Combine the salt, soda, cinnamon, oats, and flour.
3. Add the egg whites, sugar, water, and applesauce.
4. Blend in the blueberries.
5. Bake until lightly browned or about 20-25

minutes

Bran, Flaxseed, and Wheat Muffins

Servings: 24
Calories: 115.7
Prep and Cooking Time: 00:45:00

Ingredients
- 1 c of each:
  - Ground flaxseed
  - Brown sugar
  - Oat bran
  - Whole wheat flour
- 2 tsp. baking soda
- 2 tbsp cinnamon
- 1 tsp. baking powder
- ½ tsp. salt
- 1 ½ - c shredded carrots
- 2-3 apples
- ½ tsp. salt
- ¾ c 2% milk
- 2 beaten eggs
- 1 tsp. vanilla
- ½ c each (*Optional*):
  - Raisins
  - Chopped nuts

Instructions
1. Prepare 24 paper liners/oil lined muffin tin. Set the oven to 350°F.
2. Core and chop the apples.
3. Blend the sugar, bran, flaxseed, flour, and other

dry ingredients.
4. Shred the apples and carrots and toss with the nuts and raisins and all dry ingredients.
5. Whip the eggs, milk, and vanilla. Blend into the dry mixture.
6. Fill each cup ¾ full. Bake for 20 to 25 minutes.

Healthy Breakfast Cookie

Servings: 30
Calories: 111.1
Prep and Cooking Time: 00:30

Ingredients
- 2 large eggs
- ¼ c butter
- ½ c each:
  - Honey
  - Chopped - dried apricots
  - Raisins
- 1 c of each:
  - Grated carrots
  - Chopped walnuts
  - Rolled oats
  - All-purpose flour
- 1 ½ c Cheerios
- 1 tsp. each:
  - Nutmeg
  - Cinnamon

Instructions
1. Combine the egg, butter, and honey in a mixing dish. Blend in the apricots, walnuts, and raisins.

2. In a separate container, mix the cinnamon, nutmeg, flour, and oats.
3. Combine all components and add the Cheerios.
4. Drop the mixture/dough onto a baking sheet about one inch apart.
5. Bake 15 minutes or until the cookie is firm.

Pumpkin Muffins

Servings: 18
Calories: 340
Prep and Cooking Time: 00:35:00

Ingredients
- 1 can (1 pound) pumpkin
- 1 box spice cake mix
- ½ c flaxseed meal

Instructions
1. Program the temperature in the oven to 350°F.
2. Prepare a muffin tin with paper liners or cooking spray.
3. Combine all of the ingredients and bake 25 minutes.

Zucchini Bread Muffins

Servings: 24
Calories: 139.6
Prep and Cooking Time: 00:50

Ingredients
- 3 large egg whites
- 2 c of each:

- o Sugar
- o Grated zucchini
- 1 c applesauce
- 1 tbsp vanilla
- ½ tsp salt
- 2 tsp baking powder
- 3 c whole wheat flour
- 1 tsp baking soda
- 3 tsp brown sugar
- 2 tsp cinnamon

Instructions

1. Set the oven temperature to 350°F.
2. Grease 24 muffin tins with some non-stick cooking spray.
3. Combine the sugar and eggs along with the applesauce, vanilla, and zucchini.
4. Slowly, add the dry components. Mix well.
5. Empty the batter and sprinkle each one with a pinch of brown sugar.
6. Bake 20-30 minutes.

Oatmeal Dishes

Banana – Peanut Butter Oatmeal

Servings: 1
Calories: 203.5
Prep and Cooking Time: 00:05:00

Ingredients

- ½ tbsp creamy peanut butter
- ¼ c each:

○ Quick-cooking oats
○ Skim milk
- ½ of a large banana

Instructions
1. Peel and slice the banana; puree.
2. Pour the oatmeal and banana into a dish. Stir and cook for 30 seconds on high, uncovered in the microwave.
3. Stir the mixture again, and cook another 30 seconds.
4. Blend in the peanut butter.

Blue Oatmeal

Servings: 2
Calories: 214.2
Prep and Cooking Time: 00:10

Ingredients
- 2 tbsp flaxseed (ground flax)
- 1 c 100% natural whole grain oatmeal
- 2 tsp brown sugar
- 1 ½ - c water
- ½ tbsp unsweetened dry cocoa powder
- ½ c frozen - unsweetened blueberries

Instructions
1. Bring the water to boiling and dump the dry fixings into a saucepan.
2. Lower the heat and cook two to three minutes on low heat.
3. Stir in the frozen berries and enjoy.

Pumpkin Pie Oatmeal

Servings: 2
Calories: 164.2
Prep and Cooking Time: 00:25:00

Ingredients
- 1 c non-fat milk
- ½ c each:
  - Canned pumpkin
  - Uncooked old-fashioned oatmeal
- ¼ tsp pumpkin pie spice
- Pinch of ground cardamom
- 1 tbsp sugar

Instructions
1. Mix all of the ingredients listed and cook until thick; usually about 20 minutes.

Slow Cooker 6 – Grain Breakfast

Servings: 4
Calories: 134.5
Prep and Cooking Time: 8:05

Ingredients
- ¼ c rolled oats
- 2 ½ tbsp each:
  - Brown rice
  - Bulgur wheat
  - Quinoa
  - Barley
- 1 c diced apples

- 3 c water
- 1 ½ tsp ground cinnamon
- 1 tbsp vanilla extract

Instructions
1. Mix all of the fixings in the slow cooker.
2. Set the cooker on the low setting for six to eight hours.
3. Stir and add small amounts of water if desired.

Summertime Uncooked Oatmeal

Servings: 1
Calories: 391.3
Prep and Cooking Time: 00:05:00

Ingredients
- About 25 raisins
- ½ c each:
  - Milk
  - Oats
- 1 tsp cinnamon

Instructions
1. Thoroughly blend each the ingredients in a covered dish and place them in the refrigerator overnight.
2. Enjoy the next morning without any cooking.

Pancakes and Waffles

Banana Bread Pancakes

Servings: 8
Calories: 126.2
Prep and Cooking Time: 00:30

Ingredients
- 2 pouches Quaker Instant Oatmeal – Banana Bread – weight control
- 2/3 c cottage cheese
- 2 eggs or ½ c egg beaters

Garnish: Cinnamon and vanilla extract

Instructions
1. Combine all of the components for the pancakes into a blender.
2. Cook over med-high setting on the stovetop.
3. Make 8 (6 inch) pancakes and enjoy.

Cheesecake Pancakes

Servings: 2
Calories: 293.5
Prep and Cooking Time: 00:20:00

Ingredients
- 4 ounces cream cheese
- 2 large eggs
- Splenda to taste
- 1 tbsp flaxseed
- ½ tsp ground cinnamon

Instructions

1. Whisk the egg whites into stiff peaks.
2. Drop the cream cheese into a bowl and blend with the mixer until smooth. Combine this with the yolks and sweetener, flaxseed meal, salt, and cinnamon. Fold in the whipped eggs.
3. Using med-low heat, lightly grease a frying pan.
4. Use ¼ c per pancake and cook for two to three minutes per side.

Cinnamon Pancakes

Servings: 8
Calories: 92.6
Prep and Cooking Time: 00:50-01:00

Ingredients

- 1 ¼ - c whole wheat flour
- 1 tsp. baking soda
- 2 tbsp each:
  - Splenda
  - Cinnamon
- 1 tbsp vanilla extract
- ½ c egg beaters
- 1 c skim milk

Instructions

1. Combine the baking soda, flour, and Splenda in a mixing dish.
2. In another dish, blend the vanilla, milk, and eggs. Blend it into the dry ingredients (step 1). Add the cinnamon last.
3. Pour the batter into the pan 1/3 c for each

pancake.

Cottage Cheese and Oatmeal Pancakes

Servings: 6
Calories: 47.5
Prep and Cooking Time: 00:40:00 to 00:45:00

Ingredients
- 4 egg whites
- 1-2 packets Stevia
- ½ c each:
  - Dry oatmeal
  - Fat-free cottage cheese
- ½ tsp each:
  - Vanilla
  - Baking powder

Instructions
1. Add all of the ingredients into a blender except for the oats. When the mixture is smooth, slowly pour in the oats.
2. Add berries if you like, but add them after the mixture is blended.
3. Cook the pancakes until done and top with your favorite sugar-free syrup.

Oatmeal Pancakes

Servings: 4
Calories: 271.3
Prep and Cooking Time:00:35

Ingredients
- 1 ¼ c each:
  - Old Fashioned Quaker Oats
  - Skim milk
- 1 large egg
- 1 tbsp light olive oil
- 1 tsp baking powder
- 1 c whole wheat flour

Instructions
1. Mix the milk and oats in a medium dish and let them set for five minutes.
2. Add the oil and egg. Mix and add the dry ingredients.
3. Add the batter (¼ c portions) onto a lightly greased skillet. Cook until browned. Flip over and cook until done.
4. Top it off with some yogurt, maple syrup, preserves or others (not counted in nutritional counts).

Whole Wheat Applesauce Pancakes

Servings: 4
Calories: 188.3
Prep and Cooking Time: 00:35:00

Ingredients
- 1 ¼ - c. whole wheat flour
- 2 tsp. baking powder
- 9 tsp. artificial sweetener/2 tbsp sugar
- ½ tsp. salt
- 2 tbsp applesauce

- 1 c. skim milk
- 1 beaten egg

Instructions

1. Whisk all of the fixings together and cook on a hot skillet.
2. Serve and enjoy!

Sweets for Breakfast

Flax and Fruit Smoothie

Servings: 1
Calories: 428.9
Prep Time: 00:10

Ingredients

- ½ - 1 c water
- 1 scoop low-carb protein powder plain/vanilla
- ½ c coconut milk
- 1/3 c frozen strawberries/favorite
- 2 tbsp flaxseed meal
- Splenda/stevia – no carbs

Instructions

1. Combine all of the ingredients in your blender.
2. Serve right away and enjoy

Mixed Berry Smoothie

Servings: 2
Calories: 257.8
Prep Time: 00:10

Ingredients
- 1 c of each:
  - ○ Skim milk
  - ○ Fat-free yogurt
- ¾ c frozen assorted berries/your choice

Optional: ¼ c sugar

Instructions
1. Empty the yogurt and milk into a blender along with the berries.
2. Add some protein powder if you choose and enjoy.

Servings: 2
Calories: 257.8| Protein: 11.1 g | Fat: 2.8 g | Carbohydrates: 47.4 g

Mocha Banana Smoothie

Servings: 2
Calories: 170.5
Prep Time: 1:10

Ingredients
- 1 medium banana
- 1 c fat-free milk
- 1-2 tbsp honey/sugar
- 2 tbsp - instant - coffee crystals
- 1 tbsp unsweetened cocoa powder
- ½ tsp vanilla
- 1 c crushed ice/small cubes

Instructions
1. Freeze the banana for one hour and slice into ½ inch slices.
2. Combine all of the goodies in a blender, adding the ice last.
3. Enjoy when smooth.

Strawberry Smoothie

Servings: 2
Calories: 50
Prep Time: 00:10

Ingredients
- 8 ounces low-fat strawberry yogurt
- 2 c frozen strawberries
- ¾ c milk

Instructions
1. Blend all of the nutritious components and enjoy.

Yogurt Breakfast Popsicles

Servings: 6
Calories: 75
Prep Time: 04:10

Ingredients
- ½ c each:
  - Instant/regular oats
  - Skim/1% milk
- 1 c of each:
  - Greek yogurt - non-fat plain
  - Chopped fruits/mixed berries

Also Needed: Popsicle molds

Instructions

1. Combine the yogurt and milk and pour into two molds.
2. Add a few berries to each one along with half of the oatmeal.
3. Add an ice cream stick to each mold and freeze for a minimum of four hours.

Chapter 2: Salads and Sandwiches

Caprese Salad

Servings: 2
Calories: 375
Prep Time: 00:10

Ingredients
- 6 ounces strawberries
- 1 ripe avocado
- 1 (7 ounces) sliced mozzarella ball
- Small handful salad leaves
- 2-3 tbsp balsamic dressing – your choice
- Pepper and salt

Instructions
1. Toss in the salad leaves, avocado, strawberries, and cheese into a serving dish.
2. Garnish with the dressing and sprinkle with the pepper and salt. Gently toss.

California Roll in a Bowl

Servings: 4
Calories: 199.1
Prep Time: 00:15

Ingredients
- 1 head chopped lettuce
- 1 c cooked brown rice
- 1 English cucumber – seedless – thinly sliced
- 1 (8 ounces) package cooked shrimp/crabmeat – chopped
- 1 grated carrot
- 1 ripe diced avocado
- 3 tbsp pickled ginger

For the Dressing
- 1 tbsp light soy sauce
- ½ tsp wasabi powder – to taste
- 3 tbsp rice wine vinegar

Garnishes:
1 large sheet seaweed/nori (toasted and in small bits)
1 tbsp sesame seeds

Instructions
1. Combine all of the fixings for the dressing in a bowl and whisk well.
2. Divide it into four sections and enjoy.

Note: You can locate the ginger in the Asian section of the supermarket.

Caramel Apple Salad

Servings: 16
Calories: 90.7
Prep Time: 00:10

Ingredients
- 1 box butterscotch pudding mix (sugar-free instant)
- 1 tub (8 ounces) Cool Whip Free
- 1 can (14 ounces) pineapple tidbits with the juice
- 4 large each:
    - Fuji apples/Red Delicious
    - Granny Smith apples

Instructions
1. Mix the pineapple with its juice and the pudding mix in a large mixing container.
2. Dice the apples into small bits and combine with the mixture.
3. Fold in the Cool Whip, mix well, and chill.

Chickpea and Feta Salad

Servings: 1
Calories: 285.2
Prep Time: 00:15

Ingredients
- ¾ c chopped raw vegetables
- ¼ c each:
    - Can/fresh chickpeas
    - Crumbled feta cheese
- 1 tsp dried oregano
- 2 tbsp olive oil
- 1 tbsp lemon juice
- Dash each of:
    - Salt
    - Pepper

Instructions
1. Use your imagination for the chopped veggies. Include peppers, avocado, tomatoes, onions, and celery or your favorites.
2. Rinse and drain the chickpeas.
3. Combine all of the ingredients and keep it chilled in the fridge until ready to serve.

Coleslaw

Servings: 6
Calories: 71.7
Prep Time: 00:15

Ingredients
- 1 small shredded carrot
- 3 c green cabbage – shredded
- ¼ c minced onion
- 1 tbsp vinegar
- 1/3 c mayonnaise
- 2 tsp sugar
- ½ tsp each:
  - Celery seed
  - Salt

Instructions
1. Prepare the onion, carrots, and cabbage into a bowl.
2. Mix the dressing and pour over the slaw.

Cucumber and Onion Salad with Vinegar

Servings: 6
Calories: 67.5

Prep Time: 00:10

Ingredients
- Pinch of salt and pepper
- 1 red onion
- 3-5 cucumbers (peeled)
- ½ c each:
  - White vinegar
  - Water
- 1/3 c sugar

Instructions
1. Slice the cucumbers and onions very thin and add to a salad dish.
2. Combine the water, vinegar, salt, pepper, and sugar and pour over the veggies.
3. Add a cover and marinate for a minimum of one hour.

Egg Salad

Servings: 6
Calories: 115.7
Prep Time: 00:20

Ingredients
- 3 celery stalks
- 6 large hard-boiled eggs
- 2 tbsp pickle relish
- ¼ c of each:
  - Diced onions
  - Reduced fat mayonnaise
- Optional:

- ○ Pepper
- 1 tsp mustard
- Dash of each:
  - ○ Celery seed
  - ○ Paprika

Instructions
1. Peel and chop the eggs, celery, and onions.
2. Combine all of the fixings and chill in the refrigerator until ready for your meal.

Grape Salad

Servings: 16
Calories: 133.7
Prep Time: 01:30

Ingredients
- 2-4 pounds of grapes (green, red, or both)
- 1 package of fat-free– 8 ounces each:
  - ○ Sour cream
  - ○ Softened cream cheese
- ½ c each:
  - ○ Splenda/your choice
  - ○ Walnuts/pecans
- ¼ c brown sugar
- 4 tbsp vanilla extract

Instructions
1. Wash and drain the grapes.
2. Combine the sour cream, cream cheese, vanilla, and sugar—blending well for about three to four minutes on high with a mixer.

3. Toss in the grapes and toss until covered.
4. Bake in a 9x13 cake pan. Sprinkle lightly with the brown sugar. Add the nuts.
5. Chill about one hour before serving.

Israeli Salad

Servings: 8
Calories: 65.2
Prep Time: 00:10

Ingredients
- 1 medium peeled cucumber
- 3 medium tomatoes
- 1 yellow/green bell pepper
- 3 tbsp. extra-virgin olive oil
- 2 tbsp. lemon juice
- 1 tsp. of each: Salt and pepper

Instructions
1. Dice all of the veggies and combine the rest of the ingredients.

Sunshine Fruit Salad

Servings: 10
Calories: 135.2
Prep Time: 01:10

Ingredients
- 2 cans (15 ounces each) mandarin oranges in light syrup
- 3 cans (20 ounces each) pineapple chunks in 100% juice

- 2 large bananas
- 3 medium kiwi fruits – bite-sized

Instructions
1. Drain the oranges and pineapple. Reserve the pineapple juice.
2. Combine all of the fruit (omit the bananas).
3. Submerge the fruit with the juice and chill for a minimum of one hour.
4. Slice and stir in the bananas before serving.

Sandwiches

Apple and Tuna Sandwich

Servings: 3
Calories: 250
Prep Time: 00:15

Ingredients
- 1 diced apple
- 1 can (6.5ounces) packed in water – drained
- ½ tsp honey
- 1 tsp mustard
- ¼ c low-fat vanilla yogurt
- 3 lettuce leaves
- 6 slices whole wheat bread

Instructions
1. Wash, peel, and chop the apple.
2. Remove the water from the tuna and combine with the apple, honey, mustard, and yogurt in a mixing dish. Blend well.

3. Add the mixture to three slices of bread. Add the lettuce and the other slice of bread.
4. What a meal!

BBQ Steak/Chicken Wrap

Servings: 4
Calories: 405.5
Prep and Cooking Time: 00:20

Ingredients
- 8 ounces sliced - cooked steak/chicken breast
- 2 c baby spinach
- 4 (8-inch) whole wheat fat-free tortillas
- 1 c of each:
    - Frozen – thawed corn
    - Can black beans
- ½ c shredded cheese (low-fat cheddar)
- ¼ c barbecue sauce

Instructions
1. Rinse and drain the beans.
2. Program the oven temperature to 400F.
3. Lightly spray a baking dish. Roll up each of the wraps and heat thoroughly for ten minutes.

Chicken Philly Cheese Sub

Servings: 4
Calories: 409.0
Prep and Cooking Time: 00:40:00

Ingredients
- 1 pound chicken breasts

39

- 4 whole wheat hoagie rolls
- 4 slices provolone cheese
- 2 sliced bell peppers
- 1 sliced yellow onion
- 2 sliced banana peppers
- ¼ tsp black pepper
- 1 tbsp white wine vinegar

Instructions
1. Set the grill on the high setting. Flatten the meat with a mallet.
2. Grill the chicken for approximately ten minutes or until the internal temperature is at 165°F. Let it cool a few minutes and chop into ½-inch cubes.
3. Coat a saute pan with non-stick cooking spray and add the onions. Saute for five minutes on the med-high setting.
4. Add the peppers and cook another ten minutes. Pour in the vinegar while scraping up the tasty bits and remove from the pan from the burner.
5. Divide the ingredients onto the buns, and top with a cheese slice. Wrap them in foil and grill two minutes so the cheese can melt.

Grilled Cheese Pizza Sandwich

Servings: 1
Calories: 242.3
Prep and Cooking Time: 00:30

Ingredients
- 2 tbsp marinara sauce

- 2 slices mixed grain bread
- ¼ c mozzarella cheese – part skim
- Pepper and salt to taste
- 1 tsp shredded parmesan

Instructions
1. Divide the marinara sauce on each slice of bread.
2. Add the mozzarella to one with the sauce, parmesan, and add the second slice of bread.
3. Brown until the darkness you prefer.

Ranch Cheddar Turkey Burgers

Servings: 6
Calories: 155.1
Prep and Cooking Time: 00:25:00

Ingredients
- 1 (one-ounce) pouch dry ranch dressing mix
- ¼ c chopped scallion
- 1 pound lean ground turkey
- 1 c shredded cheese (low-fat)

Instructions
1. Mix all of the fixings and form six patties.
2. Cook on the grill/skillet about six to seven minutes for each side.
3. Enjoy with tomato and lettuce on a bun (not included in counts).

Tuna Salad

Ingredients
- 1 can tuna packed in water (6 ounces)
- 1 ½ tbsp mayonnaise
- 1 tbsp each:
  - Pickle juice
  - Powdered eggs

Instructions
1. Combine each of the ingredients in a blender or by hand until smooth.

Turkey Spinach Feta Burger

Servings: 6
Calories: 280
Prep and Cooking Time : 00:30

Ingredients
- 1 tbsp olive oil
- 20 ounces lean ground turkey
- 10 ounces frozen spinach
- 1 c diced red onion
- 2 minced garlic cloves
- 3 ½ ounces crumbled feta cheese
- 1 tbsp each:
  - Grilled steak seasoning (Mrs. Dash)
  - Chopped fresh oregano

Instructions
1. Thaw and drain the spinach – removing all water.
2. Saute the garlic and onion in oil, cool, and add to

a dish with the oregano, and spinach. Blend in the feta, turkey, and seasoning to form six patties.

3. Cook on the grill/stove. Place on a bun if desired, but count the calories.

Chapter 3: Main Course Meals

Beef

Bavarian Beef

Servings: 5 (5 ounces each portion)
Calories: 256.1
Prep and Cooking Time: 02:40:00

Ingredients

- 1 tbsp olive oil
- 1 ¼ pounds stewing beef
- 1 large onion
- ¾ tsp caraway seeds
- 1 bay leaf
- 1 ½ - c water
- 1/8 tsp black pepper
- ½ tsp salt
- 1 tbsp sugar
- ¼ c cider/white vinegar
- ½ small head of cabbage
- ¼ c crushed gingersnaps

Instructions

1. Cut the beef into 1-inch chunks. Thinly slice the onion. Cut the cabbage into four wedges.
2. Brown the beef in a skillet using the oil. Remove and drain the meat. Saute the onion until golden and add the meat back into the skillet.
3. Pour in the water, bay leaf, pepper, salt, and caraway

seeds.

4. Let the mixture start to boil. Lower the temperature, and cook slowly about 1 ¼ hours.
5. Add the sugar and vinegar. Stir and add the cabbage on top of the meat. Simmer the ingredients covered for another 45 minutes.
6. Transfer the cabbage and meat to a platter.
7. Strain the drippings and add adequate water to make one c of liquid. Blend in the gingersnaps to the skillet and cook until thickened.
8. Serve the sauce over the meat and veggies.

DC Sloppy Joes

Servings: 4
Calories: 162.5
Prep and Cooking Time: 00:50

Ingredients
- 16 ounces ground beef
- 1 c diet cola
- 2 tbsp each:
  - Dry mustard
  - White vinegar
- 1 tbsp Worcestershire sauce
- Garlic powder

Instructions
1. Brown the beef in a skillet, drain, and place it back into the pan.
2. Mix the remainder of the fixings with the beef and stir.
3. Cook uncovered on the low setting for 30 minutes.

Ginger Beef

Servings: 4
Calories: 207.6
Prep and Cooking Time: 00:40:00 to 01:00:00

Ingredients
- 1 pound flank steak
- 2 tbsp each:
    - Seasoned rice vinegar
    - Lite soy sauce
- 2 tsp each:
    - Corn starch
    - Ground ginger
- ½ c water
- 1 tsp garlic powder
- 10 slices fresh ginger root (1-inch diameter)
- 8 large scallions

Instructions
1. Slice the ginger into wafer thin slices, and dice. Wash and slice the scallions.
2. Mix the garlic powder, ground ginger, water, soy sauce, and vinegar.
3. Slice the meat into one-inch strips against the grain of the meat. Chill in the fridge for about 20 minutes.
4. Spray a skillet/wok with non-stick cooking oil. Using the high setting, add the veggies and meat. It should take about ten minutes to brown.
5. At the end of the cooking cycle; blend the cornstarch with some water and stir into the juices to thicken.

Ground Beef Casserole - Keema

Servings: 6
Calories: 197.3
Prep and Cooking Time: 00:30

Ingredients
- 2 c crushed tomatoes
- 1 ½ pounds lean ground sirloin
- 1 c of each:
  - Chopped onions
  - Diced potatoes
  - Frozen peas
- 1 tbsp curry powder
- ½ tsp each:
  - Ginger
  - Turmeric
  - Cinnamon
- Pepper and salt if desired

Instructions
1. Brown the onions and sirloin in a pan. Add the potatoes peas, tomatoes, and spices.
2. Simmer for 25 minutes adding a pinch of pepper and salt.
3. It should look like chili.

Ground Beef and Potato Casserole

Servings: 6-8
Calories: 166.3
Prep and Cooking Time: 01:30:00

Amy Wilson

Ingredients
- ¼ c water mixed with soup
- 1 can cream of mushroom soup (10.75 ounces)
- 1 c chopped onions
- 1 pound lean ground beef
- 3-4 medium potatoes
- ¼ tsp each:
  - Black pepper
  - Salt (optional)

Instructions
1. Program the oven to 350°F.
2. Prepare the potatoes thinly sliced with skins.
3. Brown the onions and beef; drain.
4. In a 9x11-inch (2 quarts) casserole dish, lightly spray and add a layer of potatoes and a layer of beef. Pour ½ of the soup mixture over this and add an additional layer with the rest of the ingredients. Bake one hour.
Note: Campbell's Healthy Quest was used.

Mushroom and Beef - Slow Cooker

Servings: 4
Calories: 410.5
Prep and Cooking Time: 1:30

Ingredients
- 1 pound lean stewing beef
- 1 can cream of mushroom soup (low-fat)
- 1 package dry onion soup mix
- ½ c water

- 8 ounces fresh sliced/whole mushrooms

Instructions
1. Use the medium heat setting to cook the beef in a skillet and add it to the slow cooker (four- quart size is best).
2. Add the meat on the bottom and the mushrooms. Mix the soup, water, and pour into the pot.
3. Serve over some noodles or brown rice. (Count the calories.)

Chicken and Turkey

Baked Chicken and Vegetables

Servings: 6
Calories: 240
Prep and Cooking Time: 01:10:00

Ingredients
- 6 sliced carrots
- 4 sliced potatoes
- 1 large quartered onion
- 1 skinless raw chicken
- 1 tsp thyme
- ½ c water
- ¼ tsp pepper

Instructions
1. Program the oven temperature in advance to 400°F.
2. Arrange the carrots, potatoes, and onions in a large roasting pan. Add the chicken last.

3. Combine the thyme, pepper, and water. Dump this over the ingredients in the pan.
4. Bake for one hour until brown and tender. Baste the chicken with the juices several times.

Brown Sugar Garlic Chicken

Servings: 4
Calories: 166.4
Prep and Cooking Time: 00:30

Ingredients
- 2 tbsp butter
- 12 ounces chicken breasts (no skins or bones)
- 1 garlic clove
- Black pepper

Instructions
1. Melt the butter and add the garlic in a frying pan.
2. Add the chicken with a dash of pepper and cook until done (about 15 minutes).
3. Sprinkle with the brown sugar for five minutes and serve.

Chicken and Broccoli Casserole

Servings: 4
Calories: 284.2
Prep and Cooking Time: 00:45:00

Ingredients
- 1 package (10 ounces) frozen broccoli spears
- 1 pound chicken breasts (skinless, boneless)
- 1 can cream of mushroom soup (low-sodium)

- 3 tbsp fat-free mayonnaise
- 1 c shredded (reduced fat) cheddar cheese

Instructions
1. Boil and drain the chicken breasts. When cooled, cut into one-inch bits.
2. Add the soup and mayonnaise in a casserole dish. Blend in the chicken and broccoli, mixing well.
3. Toss some cheese on top and bake for approximately 20 minutes.

Chicken Creole

Servings: 1
Calories: 269.3
Prep and Cooking Time: 00:30

Ingredients
- 4 chicken breasts – 1-inch strips – skinless and boneless
- 1 c low-sodium chili sauce
- 1 can (14 ounces) cut up tomatoes
- ½ c chopped celery
- ¼ c chopped onion
- 1 ½ c green peppers (1 large chopped)
- 2 minced garlic cloves
- 1 tbsp fresh or 1 tsp dried each:
  - Fresh parsley
  - Fresh basil
- ¼ tsp each:
  - Crushed red pepper
  - Salt

Instructions
1. Lightly grease a pan with some cooking spray.
2. Warm the pan on the high setting. Cook the chicken for three to five minutes.
3. Lower the heat and add the remainder of the ingredients.
4. Once it starts to boil, cover and simmer for ten minutes.
5. Serve over a bed of rice (calories not included in counts).

Chicken Tetrazzini

Servings: 6 (one c each)
Calories: 167
Prep and Cooking Time: 00:25:00

Ingredients
- 1 tbsp reduced calorie margarine
- 8 ounces sliced button mushrooms
- ½ c chopped scallions – approximately 5
- 3 tbsp all-purpose flour
- 1/8 tsp black pepper
- ¼ tsp garlic powder
- ½ pounds chicken breasts – cooked and cubed
- 1 c fat-free chicken broth
- ½ c fat-free skim milk
- ¼ c pimentos (2-ounce jar)
- 2 tbsp sherry cooking wine
- 8 ounces uncooked spaghetti
- 3 ½ tbsp grated parmesan cheese

Instructions
1. Break the spaghetti into thirds, cook, and drain.
2. Use a large saucepan, and combine the margarine, scallions, and mushrooms. Cook slowly for five minutes.
3. Combine the garlic powder, flour, pepper, milk, and broth in a small mixing container. Blend the mixture into the pan and continue cooking until thickened (ten minutes).
4. Blend in the chicken, sherry, and pimentos. Cook about two minutes.
5. Stir in the cheese and cooked spaghetti.

Cola Chicken

Servings: 3
Calories: 193.8
Prep and Cooking Time: 00:55

Ingredients
- 3 chicken breasts
- 1 c ketchup
- 1 can of (12 ounces) diet cola

Garnish: Chopped green onion

Instructions
1. Arrange the chicken in a frying pan. Pour in the cola and ketchup. Cover until they start boiling. Lower the temperature, and cook about 45 minutes.
2. Uncover and raise the temperature until the sauce thickens and begins to stick to the chicken.

Creamy Italian Chicken – Slow Cooker

Servings: 6 (2/3 c chicken with ½ c of rice)
Calories: 385.4
Prep and Cooking Time: 12:20:00

Ingredients
- 2 pounds chicken breasts (no skin or bones)
- ½ c water
- 1 pouch Italian dressing mix
- 1 package (8 ounces) reduced-fat cream cheese
- 1 can cream of chicken soup
- 3 c long grain rice – cooked – brown or white

Instructions
1. Arrange the breasts in the crock pot.
2. Combine the water and dressing mixture. Pour it over the chicken.
3. Secure the lid and cook on the high temperature for four hours or the low setting for eight hours. Transfer the chicken breasts to a plate.
4. In a separate dish, add the soup and cream cheese. Pour the mixture into the pot. Add all ingredients back into the cooker as you gently shred the chicken.
5. Continue cooking on low until all ingredients are heated.
6. Serve with the rice.

For Best Results: Use the lower setting, so all ingredients fully integrated.

Sour Cream and Chicken Enchiladas

Servings: 8 (2 enchiladas each)
Calories: 252.0

Ingredients
- ½ can (14.5 ounces) each:
- Fat-free cream of chicken soup
- Mexican Rotel
- 1 tbsp fresh chopped cilantro
- 1 c sour cream (fat-free)
- 12 ounces cooked shredded chicken breast
- ½ chopped white/yellow onion
- 16 corn tortillas
- 1 c shredded Colby/pepper jack cheese blend (reduced-fat)

Instructions
1. Mix the soup, sour cream, and cilantro in a saucepan. Heat and set aside.
2. Add some cooking spray to a pan. Blend the Rotel, chicken, and onions into the pan.
3. Warm the tortillas in the microwave until they are flexible.
4. Divide all of the ingredients between the tortillas and add them to a baking dish.
5. Pour the cream sauce over the tortillas along with the rest of the cheese.

Fish

BBQ Roasted Salmon

Servings: 4
Calories: 225
Prep and Cooking Time: 01:20

Ingredients
- 4 (6 ounces) salmon fillets
- 2 tbsp fresh lemon juice
- ¼ c pineapplé juice

Instructions
1. Program the oven temperature to 400°F.
2. Add the first three ingredients into a Ziploc plastic bag. Marinate for a minimum of one hour—turning occasionally.
3. Remove the salmon and throw the marinade in the trash.
4. Combine the rest of the ingredients and rub it over the fish.
5. Arrange them in a lightly coated baking dish for 12 to 15 minutes.
6. Garnish with some lemon.

Breaded Cod Fillet

Servings: 4 (six ounces each)
Calories: 150
Prep and Cooking Time: 00:20:00

Ingredients
- 4 (6 ounces) skinless cod
- Non-stick cooking spray
- ¼ tsp black pepper
- ¾ tsp fine sea salt
- 3 tbsp –divided-unsalted melted margarine
- ¼ c dried whole wheat bread crumbs
- Juice of 1 lemon – divided
- 2 tbsp chopped chives
- 3 tbsp finely chopped parsley

Instructions
1. Program the oven to 425°F.
2. Lightly coat a 9 x 13-inch casserole dish with the cooking spray.
3. Flavor the cod with the pepper and salt. Place it in the dish.
4. Drizzle half of the lemon juice and margarine on top of the cod.
5. Mix the chives, parsley, and breadcrumbs in a bowl. Sprinkle it over the cod along with the remainder of lemon and margarine.
6. Bake for approximately 12 minutes.

Broiled Tilapia Parmesan

Servings: 4
Calories: 177.1

Prep and Cooking Time: 00:15

Ingredients
- 1 pound tilapia fillets
- 1 tbsp. (+) 1 ½ tsp. reduced fat mayonnaise
- 1 tbsp. fresh lemon juice
- 2 tbsp. softened butter
- 1/8 tsp. each of:
  - Ground black pepper
  - Dried basil
  - Onion powder
  - Celery seed

Instructions
1. Preheat the broiler on the oven. Line with foil or grease a broiling pan.
2. Combine the butter, mayonnaise, parmesan cheese, and lemon juice in a small container. Add the basil, onion powder, pepper, and celery salt. Stir and set to the side.
3. Place the fillets into the baking pan and broil two to three minutes. Flip them once and broil two more minutes.
4. Take the fish from the oven and coat them with the cheese mixture. Broil two more minutes.

Mock Crab Cakes

Servings: 10
Calories: 161.4
Prep and Cooking Time: 00:40:00

Ingredients
- 2 egg whites
- 2 pounds imitation crabmeat

- 1 sleeve (34) Keebler Toasteds/or other crackers – crushed
- 4 tbsp light mayonnaise

Instructions
1. Set the oven temperature to 375°F.
2. Whisk the eggs until fluffy and blend in the mayonnaise
3. Add the crushed crackers with the eggs and combine with the crabmeat.
4. Make the patties using about ½- c for each patty.
5. Bake 15 minutes per side.

Oven-Fried Tilapia

Servings: 4 (4 ounces each)
Calories: 184.7
Prep and Cooking Time: 00:20

Ingredients
- 3 egg whites
- One pound (4) tilapia fillets
- 1 tbsp each:
  - Onion powder
  - Garlic powder
  - Grated parmesan cheese
  - Cajun seasoning
- 1 ½ c finely ground Fiber One cereal/oven-fry bread
- Non-stick cooking spray

Instructions
1. Program the oven temperature to 400°F.

2. Whisk the egg whites until frothy.
3. In a separate container, combine all of the seasonings, cheese, and cereal. Dip the fish in the egg, then the seasonings.
4. Lightly spray a cookie sheet and add the fish. Spritz a small amount of oil directly on the fish.
5. Bake 8 to 10 minutes.

Salmon in a Jiffy

Servings: 4 (3 ounces each)
Calories: 183.1
Prep and Cooking Time: 01:25:00

Ingredients
- 12 ounces fresh salmon
- ¼ c each soy sauce
- Maple syrup/honey (not pancake syrup)
- 2-3 minced garlic cloves

Instructions
1. Combine all of the fixings into a Ziploc bag and shake. Open the bag, and put the salmon in the marinade. Leave it in the fridge for at least an hour.
2. Add everything into a casserole dish and cover with foil.
3. Bake for 15 minutes at 350°F.

Salmon Patties

Servings: 4
Calories: 216.8

Prep and Cooking Time: 00:30

Ingredients
- 1 celery stalk
- ¼ c bell pepper - green
- ½ medium onion
- 1 can pink salmon
- ½ c breadcrumbs
- 1 egg
- ½ tsp each:
  - Chili powder
  - *Optional*: Old Bay Seasoning

Instructions
1. Chop the pepper, onion, and celery into fine bits.
2. Clean the salmon by discarding the bones and skin.
3. Mix the egg, veggies, breadcrumbs, salmon, and seasonings together. Scoop them out to make four patties, and add to a well-greased griddle.
4. Smash the patty and cook five minutes per side.
5. Top with a bit of ketchup or horseradish.

Pork

Asian Pork Tenderloin

Servings: 8 (4 ounces each)
Calories: 256
Baking Time : 00:40

Ingredients

- 1/3 c each of:
    - Brown sugar
    - Light soy sauce
- 2 tbsp each:
    - Rice vinegar
    - Worcestershire sauce
    - Lemon juice
- 1 tbsp each of:
    - Ginger
    - Dry mustard
- 1 ½ tsp pepper
- 4 minced garlic cloves
- 2 lbs. pork tenderloin

Instructions

1. Add all of the ingredients into a freezer bag along with the tenderloin. Set the mixture in the refrigerator overnight.
2. Program the oven to 375°F.
3. When ready for the meal, bake for 30 to 40 minutes.
4. *Note*: You can also use the slow cooker for four to six hours.

BBQ Pulled Pork Roast – Slow Cooker

Servings: 12
Calories: 296.9
Prep and Cooking Time: 07:20:00

Ingredients

- 1 c of each:
    - Chopped onions

- ○ Chopped celery
- ○ Water
- ○ Barbecue sauce
- ○ Ketchup
- 2 tbsp each:
  - ○ Worcestershire sauce
  - ○ Vinegar
  - ○ Brown sugar
- 1 tsp each:
  - ○ Salt
  - ○ Chili powder
- ½ tsp each:
  - ○ Garlic powder
  - ○ Pepper
- 3 pounds boneless pork roast

Instructions
1. Mix all of the ingredients in the slow cooker.
2. Arrange the roast in the pot last.
3. Cover and cook for six to seven hours on high.
4. Arrange the meat on a platter, shred it, and add it back into the pot. Simmer until hot and enjoy.

Caribbean Pork

Servings: 4
Calories: 246.2
Prep and Cooking Time : 01:00

Ingredients
- 1 (12 ounces) boneless pork loin
- 2 tbsp flour
- 1 tbsp each:

- ○ Canola oil
- ○ Worcestershire sauce
- 1 minced garlic clove
- 1 medium sliced onion
- 1 c water
- 1 (seeded chopped) green bell pepper
- 1 small chili pepper (seeded - minced)
- 1 can (8 ounces) sliced pineapple in juice
- ½ tsp ground ginger
- ¾ tsp salt
- ¼ - tsp freshly ground black pepper
- 1 large (diced - seeded) tomato
- ½ medium cucumber (peeled, seeded, and diced)

Instructions

1. Remove all fat from the meat and slice into one-inch cubes. Toss in the flour.
2. Heat a skillet (med-high), and coat it with cooking spray. Cook the chicken about five minutes, browning each side. Place the cooked chicken on a plate.
3. Pour the oil into the pan and saute the onion and garlic, along with the green and chili peppers for about five minutes.
4. Place the chicken back into the pan and add the water, salt, pepper, ginger, and Worcestershire sauce. Drain the juices from the pineapple and add into the mixture.
5. Place a top on the pan, reduce the heat, and continue cooking for about 30 minutes.
6. Cut the pineapple slices into eight segments. Add the tomato, fruit, and cucumber to the stew. Continue simmering without the lid for about ten

more minutes.

Grilled Honey Garlic Pork Chops

Servings: 6
Calories: 204.3
Prep and Cooking Time: 00:30:00

Ingredients
- 3 tbsp soy sauce
- ¼ (+) 1/8 c honey
- 6 boneless fat-free pork loin chops
- 6 minced garlic cloves

Instructions
1. Blend the soy sauce, garlic, and honey. Evenly cover the chops.
2. Save the honey mix for basting.
3. Grill over med-high heat with a closed lid.

Mustard Brown Sugar Pork Chops

Servings: 6
Calories: 228.1
Prep and Cooking Time: 00:35

Ingredients
- 1/3 c yellow mustard
- ½ c brown sugar
- 6 boneless pork loin chops

Instructions
1. Blend the sugar and mustard together and pour

over the chops.

2. Bake 25 minutes at 350°F.

Chapter 4: Stir Fry, Vegetable Noodles, Soups, and Stews

Pasta Dishes

Mac and Cheese – Butternut Pasta

Servings: 8
Calories: 230
Prep and Cooking Time: 01:40:00

Ingredients
- 1 pound butternut squash
- 1 ½ c skim milk
- 1 c vegetable broth (low-sodium)
- Pinch each of:
  - Freshly ground black pepper
  - Cayenne pepper
  - Nutmeg
- ¾ tsp salt
- 1 c shredded cheese (extra sharp)
- 1 pound whole wheat spirals
- ½ c ricotta (part-skim) cheese
- 4 tbsp grated parmesan cheese
- 1 tsp olive oil
- 2 tbsp breadcrumbs
- Cooking spray for pan

Instructions
1. Program the oven setting to 375°F.

2. Peel, deseed, and dice the squash. Add the milk and stock to a saucepan over med-high heat. Mash and stir in the pepper, salt, cayenne, and nutmeg. Lower the heat to medium and cook slowly for ten minutes.
3. Prepare the noodles in a large pot of water, cooking about eight minutes. Drain and add them to a square baking dish coated with some olive oil spray. Blend in the noodle mix and stir.
4. Combine the rest of the parmesan, breadcrumbs, and oil - to crush and add to the top of the noodles.
5. Bake about 20 minutes covered with foil. Discard the foil and cook 20-40 more minutes.

Mediterranean Salmon with Pasta

Servings: 4
Calories: 407.5
Prep and Cooking Time: 00:30

Ingredients
- 4 (4 ounces) salmon fillets (16 ounces total)
- 2 medium sliced tomatoes
- 1 medium red bell pepper
- 4 c whole wheat spaghetti - cooked
- *To Taste*:
  - Black pepper
  - Lemon juice
  - 2 tbsp prepared pesto

Garnish: Drizzle of olive oil

Instructions
1. Slice the peppers into thin slices.

2. Program the oven setting to 400°F.
3. Arrange each of the fillets on the center of aluminum foil along with ½ tbsp of the pesto sauce. Divide the veggies on/around the fish. Sprinkle with pepper and enclose the foil.
4. Bake 15 to 20 minutes.

Not Fried Rice

Servings: 4 – One c each
Calories: 199
Prep and Cooking Time: 00:15:00

Ingredients
- 2 slightly beaten eggs
- 2 c long grain rice – cooked
- 2 chopped carrots
- 1 chopped celery stalk
- 1 small chopped onion
- ½ c each frozen:
    - Corn
    - Peas
- 2 tbsp soya sauce

As Needed: Water

Instructions
1. Cook the egg into an omelet using the med-high setting on the wok, and set aside.
2. Toss in the onion, celery, and carrots and stir fry until the veggies become crispy and tender.
3. Cut up the omelet and add it with the corn and peas. Add the soya sauce and rice.
4. Combine and enjoy.

Peanut and Sesame Noodles

Servings: 4
Calories: 208.2
Prep and Cooking Time: 00:20

Ingredients
- 2 c whole wheat spaghetti – cooked
- 3 tbsp each:
    - Smooth peanut butter
    - Hot water
- 1 tbsp each:
    - Freshly chopped ginger
    - Sesame oil
    - Red wine vinegar
    - Toasted sesame seeds
- 1 tsp red pepper flakes
- 1 chopped garlic clove
- 1 tsp red pepper flakes
- 2 tbsp soy sauce

Instructions
1. Prepare the spaghetti and drain.
2. Combine the other components until the peanut butter has dissolved.
3. Add the sauce to the pasta and sprinkle with the sesame seeds.

Shrimp Pasta

Servings: 6
Calories: 363.5
Prep and Cooking Time: 00:15:00

Ingredients
- 1 pound fresh medium shrimp
- 8 ounces fettuccine
- 1 package reduced-fat cream cheese (8 ounces)
- 1 c of each:
  - Chicken broth
  - Grated parmesan cheese
- 2 garlic cloves
- 5 ounces frozen spinach – thawed – moisture removed

To Taste: Pepper and salt

Instructions
1. Prepare the fettuccine.
2. Heat a skillet using the med-high setting. Add the chicken broth and cream cheese. Cook while stirring three to four minutes until it's well blended.
3. Add the garlic, pepper, and salt, along with the parmesan cheese.
4. Stir in the shrimp and stir until completely done. Toss in the spinach, stir, and enjoy.

Protein: 30.9g | Fat: 15.2 g | Carbohydrates: 24.0 g

Skillet Lasagna

Servings: 6
Calories: 342.3
Prep and Cooking Time: 00:35

Ingredients
- 1 small chopped onion

- 1 pound lean ground beef
- 3 minced garlic cloves
- 8 ounces tomato sauce
- 1 can (14 ounces) diced tomatoes
- 1 ¼ - c water
- 2 ½ c broken whole wheat lasagna noodles
- 1 tsp each:
    - Oregano leaves
    - Salt
    - Basil leaves
    - Parsley flakes
- 1 egg
- 1 c fat-free cottage cheese
- ¼ c grated parmesan cheese (fat-free)

Optional: Pepper and dried basil
Garnish: Shredded mozzarella cheese

Instructions

1. Brown the garlic, onions, and beef in a large skillet. Drain and add the tomatoes, sauce, water, salt, oregano, basil, and parsley. Stir, add the noodles, and bring to a boil.
2. Reduce the heat and simmer, covered, for 20 minutes.
3. Blend in the parmesan and cottage cheese along with the egg.
4. Sprinkle with the pepper and basil.
5. Arrange a rounded tbsp of the cheese mix onto the pasta.
6. Place a top on the pot and continue cooking for five minutes. Sprinkle with the mozzarella and enjoy.

Vegetarian Stuffed Shells

Servings: 4
Calories: 281.0
Prep and Cooking Time: 00:40:00

Ingredients
- 12 jumbo pasta shells
- 4 ounces fat-free cream cheese
- 6 ounces fat-free cottage cheese
- 1 c each of:
  - Chopped mushrooms
  - Fat-free shredded mozzarella
- 3 tsp granulated garlic
- 2 c marinara sauce
- ½ tsp dried rosemary
- ½ tbsp each:
  - Dried parsley
  - Dried oregano

Instructions
1. Preheat the oven to 350°F.
2. Cook the shells, drain, and rinse under cold water.
3. Combine the cheeses, spices, and mushrooms—mixing well.
4. Pack the shells and arrange each one on an oven-safe container.
5. Pour the marinara over the shells, cover, and bake for about 20 minutes.

Stir Fry

Apple Pork Stir Fry

Servings: 4 (2 ounces of pork each)
Calories: 312.8
Prep and Cooking Time: 00:15:00

Ingredients
- ½ pound pork tenderloin
- 2 tbsp each:
  - Peach jam
  - Reduced-sodium soy sauce
  - Water
- ½ tsp cornstarch
- 1 tbsp fresh ginger root- minced
- 1 ½ tsp each:
  - Sesame oil - dark
  - Canola oil
- 1 c each bell peppers:
  - Yellow
  - Red
  - Green
- 1 can (8 ounces) sliced and drained water chestnuts
- ½ c scallions
- Freshly ground black pepper
- 2 firm apples – Gala or Fuji

Instructions
1. Finely chop the ginger and scallion. Slice the pork into thin strips and cut the apples into one-inch pieces.
2. Mix the water, cornstarch, soy sauce, and jam in a

small dish.

3. Heat the sesame oil using medium-high heat in a large pan. Toss in the ginger and pork – stir fry until browned, usually about three to five minutes. Add the ginger and pork to a dish.

4. Pour the canola oil into the pan along with the apples, chestnuts, and peppers and stir-fry for about three minutes.

5. Add the pork back in the pan for 30 seconds and add the jam mix to the pan, stirring another 30 seconds. Sprinkle with the pepper.

Chicken Broccoli and Tomato Stir Fry

Servings: 4
Calories: 177.8
Prep and Cooking Time: 00:10:00

Ingredients
- 1 pound boneless chicken breast (1-inch chunks)
- 2 tsp canola oil
- ¼ tsp salt
- 1 tsp fresh ginger –finely chopped or 1/4 tsp ground ginger
- 2 tsp finely chopped garlic
- 1 tbsp soy sauce
- 3 c broccoli florets
- 4 firm plum tomatoes (quartered lengthwise)
- 1 c (divided) reduced-sodium chicken broth
- 1 tbsp cornstarch

Instructions
1. Use a wok or 12-inch skillet over medium-high heat. Add the oil and chopped breast of chicken

and cook three minutes.

2. Pour in the ginger, soy sauce, and garlic. Stir and add the broccoli and ½ c of the chicken broth. Cover and cook two to three more minutes.

3. Mix the remainder of the broth and cornstarch until dissolved. Add it and the tomatoes to the skillet.

4. Reduce the heat setting to med-low and continue cooking for about two minutes.

Chinese Stir Fry

Servings: 1
Calories: 243.2
Prep and Cooking Time: 00:15:00

Ingredients

- 5.5 ounces Chicken/Beef/Pork
- 1 tbsp each:
  - Low –sodium soy sauce
  - Minced garlic/powdered garlic
  - Rice wine
- 1/8 tsp sugar
- 1 tsp each:
  - Ginger powder
  - Corn starch
- ¼ c chopped onion
- ½ tbsp olive oil
- 2 straws - chopped green onion
- 4-5 thin slices fresh ginger
- ½ tbsp reduced-sodium garlic sauce
- 3 c chopped vegetables (green peppers, mushroom, snow peas, bok choy, etc.)

Instructions
1. Combine the soy sauce, ginger powder, garlic, rice wine, sugar, and cornstarch in a dish with your choice of meat.
2. In a large pan over medium heat, add the oil and onion. Saute for one minute and add the meat. When browned slightly, add the ginger slices and onion.
3. Saute three to five minutes.
4. Place hard veggies in one dish and the delicate/leafy ones in another. Pour in the garlic sauce, soy sauce and a sprinkle of powdered ginger to the veggies. Add them to the pan (crunchy ones first).
5. Add the leafy veggies last and cook until wilted.

Note: Use yellow wine for chicken/white wine for beef and pork.

Hawaiian Chicken Stir Fry

Servings: 6 (1 c stir fry (+) ¾ c cooked rice)
Calories: 330
Prep and Cooking Time: 01:00:00

Ingredients
- 2 tbsp soy sauce
- 1 tbsp cornstarch
- 2 c pineapple in 100% juice (reserve the juice)
- 1 tsp chicken bouillon
- 10 ounces frozen stir-fry vegetables
- ¾ c frozen snap peas
- 3 (4.8 ounces) cubed chicken breasts
- 1 ½ c uncooked whole grain brown rice

Instructions
1. *Prepare the Rice*: Pour 3 ½ c of water in a pan, and wait for it to boil. Pour in the rice. Cover and cook 45 minutes/until the water is completely engrossed.
2. *The Stir Fry*: Cube and cook the chicken until browned.
3. Mix one c pineapple juice (plus enough water to make the one c), soy sauce, bouillon, and cornstarch. Pour the juice over the chicken.
4. Stir in the veggies and stir until juice has thickened.
5. Add the pineapple and cook three minutes.
6. Serve over ¾ c of brown rice.

Slimmer Beef Stroganoff - Stir Fry

Servings: 1
Calories: 514.5
Prep and Cooking Time:00:15

Ingredients
- 1 ½ - c whole wheat bow tie pasta
- 1 pound beef tenderloin tips
- 1/3 c chopped onion
- ½ pound sliced mushrooms
- 2 tsp olive oil
- 1 can (10.5 ounces) beef broth
- 2 tbsp whole wheat flour

Instructions
1. Prepare the pasta.
2. Cut the beef into one-inch cubes and trim away all

fat.

3. Lightly grease a skillet with some cooking spray. Add the beef and stir-fry for three to five minutes using medium heat. Transfer to a dish.
4. In the same pan add the oil, onions, and mushrooms. Cook for two to three minutes.
5. Blend in the flour and broth stirring until blended.
6. Once it begins to boil, cook for about two minutes. Add pepper and salt.

Spicy Stir Fry Scallops

Servings: 4
Calories: 153.8
Prep and Cooking Time: 00:10:00

Ingredients
- 1 ½ tbsp olive oil
- 5-6 ounces frozen vegetables
- 12 ounces scallops
- 1 c diced tomatoes
- 1 tbsp teriyaki sauce
- ¼ tsp crushed red pepper flakes

Instructions
1. Add the oil to a wok using high heat.
2. Toss in the scallops for one minute.
3. Add the tomatoes and frozen veggies and stir fry about two to three minutes.
4. Pour in the sauce and pepper flakes.

Soups

Cabbage Vegetable Soup

Servings: 6 (1 ½ c each)
Calories: 165.2
Prep and Cooking Time: 00:30:00

Ingredients
- 1 medium diced onion
- 1 can each:
    - 28 ounces - crushed tomatoes
    - 14.5 ounces green beans
    - 15 ounces can pinto beans
    - 12 ounces sweet yellow corn
- 3 medium diced carrots
- 1 head shredded cabbage
- 3 diced stalks of celery

Instructions
1. Pour the tomatoes, cabbage, celery, onion, and carrots in a pot. Simmer about 20 minutes over medium heat.
2. Add the canned veggies and serve.

Eggplant Stew

Servings: 10
Calories: 61.6
Prep and Cooking Time: 01:40:00

Ingredients
- 1 ½ pounds eggplant
- 2-3 sliced summer squash

- 3-4 sliced zucchini
- 8 ounces sliced mushrooms
- 1 tsp crushed garlic
- 1 tbsp olive oil
- 1 coarsely chopped onion
- 1 can (15 ounces) diced tomatoes
- *Optional*: 1 can of chickpeas
- 1 tbsp chili powder/Szechuan sauce
- Pepper and salt to taste

Instructions

1. Cut the peeled/unpeeled eggplant into 2-inch cubes.
2. Add the oil, onion, and garlic to a stew pot (10-12 quarts), and saute five to ten minutes. Toss in the mushrooms and cook another five to ten minutes. Dump the tomatoes into the pot and heat until it bubbles.
3. Lower the heat source, and cook for 45 minutes and mix in the squash and zucchini. Cook 30 additional minutes and add the spices along with the chickpeas if used.
4. Serve it hot.

Fifteen Minute Chili

Servings: 4
Calories: 370.8

Ingredients
- ½ c chopped onions
- 1 pound ground turkey
- 1 can (16 ounces) each:

  - ○ Pinto beans
  - ○ Kidney beans
- 1 can of (28 ounces) chopped stewed tomatoes
- 1 tbsp each:
  - ○ Cumin powder
  - ○ Chili powder
- ½ c salsa

Instructions
1. Rinse and drain the kidney and pinto beans.
2. Brown the onions and turkey in a large pot.
3. Empty the tomatoes, beans, cumin, salsa, chili powder, and garlic into the pot. Cook until boiling and serve.
4. Garnish with some cheese (count the carbs).

5 Ingredient Soup

Servings: 10
Calories: 128.0
Prep and Cooking Time: 00:25:00
Ingredients
- 1 can of each (14.4 ounces):
  - ○ Corn – drained and rinsed
  - ○ Fat-free chicken broth
  - ○ Diced tomatoes (no-salt added)
  - ○ Fat-free refried beans
  - ○ Black beans - drained and rinsed

Instructions
1. Combine all of the above ingredients using a whisk to blend in the refried beans.
2. Simmer and serve.

3. Garnish with some avocado, green onions, or sour cream.

French Onion Soup

Servings: 2
Calories: 165.9
Prep and Cooking Time: 00:30:00

Ingredients
- 1 medium yellow onion
- ¼ c water
- 4 c beef broth
- ½ c part-skim mozzarella cheese – shredded
- 2 slices whole-wheat bread

Instructions
1. Toss the onion into boiling water, and continue cooking until the onions are translucent.
2. Pour in the beef broth and cook another 15 to 20 minutes
3. Add it to two c. Garnish each one with one ounce of shredded mozzarella and one tbsp of croutons.
4. Place it under the broiler and melt the cheese, if you like it that way.

Southwestern Chicken Soup

Servings: 8 (one c servings)
Calories: 270.5
Prep and Cooking Time: 00:25:00

Ingredients
- 1 pound chicken breasts (16 ounces) bite-sized

pieces
- 1 small chopped onion
- 3 chopped garlic cloves
- 1 jalapeno pepper –chopped
- 4 c fresh spinach /4 ounces frozen
- 1 chopped green pepper
- 1 tbsp each:
  - Olive oil
  - Cumin
- 2 chopped avocados
- 1 can (14 ounces) each:
  - Low-sodium chopped tomatoes
  - Pinto/black beans – drained and rinsed
- ¼ c cilantro – torn
- 2 limes – juiced
- 2 c cooked brown rice
- 1-quart chicken stock

Instructions
1. Prepare the rice and heat the oil over medium heat. Toss in garlic, peppers, and onion. Cook approximately five minutes.
2. Lower the temperature setting to medium and add the tomatoes. Simmer about ten minutes.
3. Take the pan off the burner and blend in the lime juice, mixing well. Add salt and pepper if desired.
4. Add ½ c of rice to each bowl and garnish with a sprinkle of avocado and cilantro.

Note: Leave the seeds in the jalapeno for more spice.

Tomato Soup

Servings: 8
Calories: 98.9
Prep and Cooking Time: 00:25:00

Ingredients
- 1 c chopped yellow/white onion
- 3 minced garlic cloves
- 2 tbsp olive oil
- 2 pounds tomatoes
- ¼ tsp red pepper flakes
- 1 tbsp brown sugar
- ½ tsp dried thyme
- 4 small slices of bread
- 1 tbsp balsamic vinegar
- 1 ½ c chicken/vegetable stock (low-sodium)

Instructions
1. Remove the seeds and chop the tomatoes. Discard the crust from the bread.
2. Add the oil to a stock pot along with the garlic and onions. Saute five minutes.
3. Blend in the tomatoes, thyme, sugar, pepper, and bread. Cook for three minutes.
4. Puree with a food processor/immersion blender.
5. Slowly add the stock and simmer for 10 minutes. Add the vinegar and cook approximately two minutes.

Chapter 5: Veggies, Sides, and Casseroles

Black Bean and Rice Casserole

Servings: 8
Calories: 267
Prep and Cooking Time: 01:30:00

Ingredients
- 1/3 c each:
  - Diced onion
  - Brown rice
- 1 c vegetable broth
- 1 tbsp olive oil
- 1 lb. chopped chicken breast (no skin or bones)
- 1 medium thinly sliced zucchini
- ½ c sliced mushrooms
- ¼ tsp cayenne pepper
- ½ tsp cumin
- 1 can of (4 ounces) diced green chilies
- 1/3 c shredded carrots
- 1 can of (15 ounces) drained black beans
- 2 c shredded Swiss cheese

Instructions
1. Prepare a pot with the vegetable broth and rice, bringing it to a boil. Lower the heat setting and cook covered on low for 45 minutes.
2. Program the oven temperature to 350°F.
3. Spray a baking dish with some cooking spray.

4. Heat the oil in a pan. Use medium heat and toss in the onion and cook until tender. Add the chicken, zucchini, mushrooms, and seasonings. Continue cooking until the zucchini is lightly browned.

5. In a large mixing dish, combine the onion, cooked rice, chicken, zucchini, beans, chilies, mushrooms, one c of Swiss cheese, and the carrots.

6. Empty the ingredients into the casserole dish along with the remainder of the Swiss cheese as a topping. Cover and bake 30 minutes. Uncover, and continue cooking ten more minutes.

Broccoli Casserole

Servings: 12
Calories: 90.5
Prep and Cooking Time: 00:30:00

Ingredients
- 4 c cut up broccoli
- 1 sleeve Ritz crackers
- 2 c cheddar cheese

Instructions
1. Add the casserole ingredients into a Pyrex dish with the crumbled crackers on top.
2. Bake long enough to melt the cheese at 375°F.

Cheesy Stuffed Acorn Squash

Servings: 4
Calories: 299
Prep and Cooking Time: 00:45:00

Ingredients
- 1 pound ground turkey breast (extra-lean)
- 2 acorn squash
- 1 can (8 ounces) tomato sauce
- 1 c each:
  - Sliced fresh mushrooms
  - Chopped onion
  - Diced celery
- 1 tsp each:
  - Garlic powder
  - Basil
  - Oregano
- 1 pinch black pepper
- 1/8 tsp salt
- 1 c shredded cheddar cheese (reduced-fat)

Instructions
1. Program the oven temperature to 350°F.
2. Slice the squash in half and remove the seeds. Arrange the squash, cut side down, in a dish and microwave on high for 20 minutes.
3. Brown the turkey in a skillet and add the onion and celery. Saute two to three minutes. Blend in the mushrooms, and add the sauce and seasonings. Divide into quarters and spoon into the squash.
4. Cover and bake for 15 minutes.
5. Garnish with the cheese and bake until the cheese has melted.

Grilled Veggies and Pineapples

Servings: 6
Calories: 136.5
Prep and Cooking Time: 00:40:00

Ingredients
- 1 c of each:
  - Diced potatoes
  - Bell peppers
  - Raw mushrooms
- 1 c cherry tomatoes
- 1 medium chopped onion
- 1 can of pineapple chunks – natural juices
- 2 tsp each:
  - Dill weed
  - Chopped garlic
- 1 tsp celery seed/salt
- 3 tbsp olive oil
- 1 ½ tsp each: *Optional*:
- Onion powder
- Cayenne pepper
- Garlic powder
- Pepper and salt to taste

Instructions

1. *Chop the veggies*
2. *Option 1*: Add the veggies on a piece of oil-sprayed foil. Arrange the package on the grill using medium heat for 20-25 minutes (turning every five minutes).
3. *Option 2*: Place the veggies on wooden skewers

that have been soaked in water. Cook on a med-high grill turning every five minutes or so.

4. *Oven:* Bake at 400°F, checking every 10 minutes.

Mini Eggplant Pizzas

Servings: 4
Calories: 119.1
Prep and Cooking Time: 00:30:00

Ingredients
- 4 tsp olive oil
- 1 eggplant (3-inches in diameter)
- ¼ c pasta sauce
- 1/8 tsp black pepper
- ½ tsp salt
- ½ c shredded mozzarella cheese (part-skim)

Instructions
1. Set the temperature of the toaster oven/oven to 425°F.
2. Peel and cut the eggplant into 4 (1/2-inch) slices. Brush them with oil, pepper, and salt.
3. Bake for six to eight minutes – turning once.
4. Add the sauce and top with the cheese and bake three to five minutes.

Spinach Lasagna

Servings: 8
Calories: 316.8
Prep and Cooking Time 02:00:00

Ingredients
- 1 large 3gg
- 2 c cottage cheese (1% milkfat)
- 2 c part-skim mozzarella cheese
- 10 ounces baby spinach
- 1 jar spaghetti/marinara tomato sauce
- 1 c water
- 9 lasagna noodles
- 1/8 tsp black pepper

Instructions
1. Program the oven temperature to 350°F.
2. Combine the thawed, drained spinach, one c of mozzarella, cottage cheese, egg, and the seasonings in a large mixing bowl.
3. Spray a 9x13x2-inch casserole dish with some cooking spray.
4. Layer ½ c of the sauce, 3 noodles, and ½ of the cheese mixture. Repeat, and top with the noodles one c of mozzarella. Pour water around the edges and toothpicks on top to place a piece of foil over the noodles.
5. Bake covered for one hour to 1 ½ hours. Let it rest 15 minutes.

Sweet Potato Spicy Fries

Servings: 4
Calories: 116.9
Prep and Cooking Time 00:30:00

Ingredients
- 1 ½ tbsp olive oil

- 2 medium sweet potatoes
- ¼ tsp salt
- 1 tsp ground cumin
- ½ tsp each:
  - Onion powder
  - Chili powder

Instructions

1. Program the oven setting to 450°F.
2. Wash and cut the potatoes lengthwise into fry strips. Combine all ingredients together in a dish and shake
3. Arrange them on a baking sheet on some parchment paper or foil.
4. Bake and turn every 5 to 6 minutes - for a total of 20 minutes cooking time.

Vegetarian Chili

Servings: 8
Calories: 279.8
Prep and Cooking Time 11:17:00

Ingredients

- 1 can (15 ounces) each:
  - Pinto beans
  - Black beans
  - Light red kidney beans
  - Dark red kidney beans
- 1 can (28 ounces) diced tomatoes
- 2 cans (28 ounces) crushed tomatoes
- 3 c celery
- 1 medium red onion

- 1 small diced each of:
    - Red bell pepper
    - Yellow bell pepper
- 4 tbsp chili powder
- 3 tbsp garlic powder
- 2 tbsp ground cumin

Instructions
1. Drain and rinse all of the beans. Dice the veggies.
2. Lightly spray a large pan over medium heat and cook the veggies about six to seven minutes or until they are softened.
3. Combine the spices, beans, and tomatoes in a slow cooker (6-7 hours on low) or a Dutch oven (3-4 hours on low).

Conclusion

Thank for making it through to the end of your copy of Gastric Sleeve Cookbook (R): Carefully Selected Easy to Make Recipes; Healthy and Delicious for LEGENDS After Gastric Surgery. All The Best Have Lovely Taste! Let's hope it was informative and provided you with all of the tools you need to achieve your goals whatever they may be.

The next step is to plan your meals and get the cabinets stocked with all of the ingredients you will need to change your way of eating and make healthier choices.

Finally, if you found this book useful in any way, a review on Amazon is always appreciated!

Index

Chapter 1: Breakfast Goodies

- <u>Cottage Cheese and Oatmeal Pancakes</u>
- <u>Oatmeal Pancakes</u>
- <u>Whole Wheat Applesauce Pancakes</u>

Sweets for Breakfast
- <u>Flax and Fruit Smoothie</u>
- <u>Mixed Berry Smoothie</u>
- <u>Mocha Banana Smoothie</u>
- <u>Strawberry Smoothie</u>
- <u>Yogurt Breakfast Popsicles</u>

Chapter 2: Salads and Sandwiches
- Caprese Salad
- California Roll in a Bowl
- Caramel Apple Salad
- Chickpea and Feta Salad
- Coleslaw
- Cucumber and Onion Salad with Vinegar
- Egg Salad
- Grape Salad
- Israeli Salad
- Sunshine Fruit Salad

Sandwiches
- Apple and Tuna Sandwich
- BBQ Steak/Chicken Wrap
- Chicken Philly Cheese Sub
- Grilled Cheese Pizza Sandwich
- Ranch Cheddar Turkey Burgers
- Turkey Spinach Feta Burger

Chapter 3: Main Course
Beef
- Bavarian Beef
- DC Sloppy Joes
- Ginger Beef
- Ground Beef Casserole – Keema
- Ground Beef and Potato Casserole
- Mushroom and Beef – Slow Cooker

Chicken and Turkey
- Baked Chicken and Vegetables
- Brown Sugar Garlic Chicken
- Chicken and Broccoli Casserole

- Chicken Creole
- Chicken Tetrazzini
- Cola Chicken
- Creamy Italian Chicken – Slow Cooker
- Sour Cream and Chicken Enchiladas

Fish
- BBQ Roasted Salmon
- Breaded Cod Fillet
- Broiled Tilapia Parmesan
- Mock Crab Cakes
- Oven-Fried Tilapia
- Salmon in a Jiffy
- Salmon Patties

Pork
- Asian Pork Tenderloin
- BBQ Pulled Pork Roast – Slow Cooker
- Caribbean Pork
- Grilled Honey Garlic Pork Chops
- Mustard Brown Sugar Pork Chops

Chapter 4: Stir Fry, Vegetable Noodles, Soups, & Stews

Pasta Dishes
- Mac and Cheese – Butternut Squash
- Mediterranean Salmon with Pasta
- Not Fried Rice
- Peanut and Sesame Noodles
- Shrimp Pasta

Description

This is a must for your personal library, the Gastric Sleeve Cookbook (R): Carefully Selected Easy to Make Recipes; Healthy and Delicious for LEGENDS After Gastric Surgery. All The Best Have Lovely Taste!

You will soon discover within the pages of this cookbook that you are truly entering a new stage of your life. You have the tools to continue down the right path to a much healthier future.

These are just a few of the tastes to tempt you:

- Cottage Cheese and Oatmeal Pancakes
- Mediterranean Salmon with Pasta
- Cheesy Stuffed Acorn Squash
- Fifteen Minute Chili
- Hawaiian Chicken Stir Fry

So many more!

You know what to do to own this great collection.

Happy Cooking!

Made in the USA
Middletown, DE
08 January 2018